Francis Frith's
Yorkshire

Photographic Memories

Francis Frith's
Yorkshire

Revised edition of original work by

Clive Hardy

First published in the United Kingdom in 1998
by WBC Ltd

Hardback Reprinted in 2000
ISBN 1-85937-290-2

British Library Cataloguing in Publication Data

Francis Frith's Yorkshire
Clive Hardy

Frith Book Company Ltd
Frith's Barn, Teffont,
Salisbury, Wiltshire SP3 5QP
Tel: +44 (0) 1722 716 376
Email: info@frithbook.co.uk
www.frithbook.co.uk

Printed and bound in Great Britain

Front cover: Knaresborough, Market Day 1921 71687

AS WITH ANY HISTORICAL DATABASE THE FRITH ARCHIVE IS CONSTANTLY BEING CORRECTED AND IMPROVED
AND THE PUBLISHERS WOULD WELCOME INFORMATION ON OMISSIONS OR INACCURACIES

Contents

Francis Frith: *Victorian Pioneer*

FRANCIS FRITH, Victorian founder of the world-famous photographic archive, was a complex and multitudinous man. A devout Quaker and a highly successful Victorian businessman, he was both philosophic by nature and pioneering in outlook.

By 1855 Francis Frith had already established a wholesale grocery business in Liverpool, and sold it for the astonishing sum of £200,000, which is the equivalent today of over £15,000,000. Now a multi-millionaire, he was able to indulge his passion for travel. As a child he had pored over travel books written by early explorers, and his fancy and imagination had been stirred by family holidays to the sublime mountain regions of Wales and Scotland. 'What a land of spirit-stirring and enriching scenes and places!' he had written. He was to return to these scenes of grandeur in later years to 'recapture the thousands of vivid and tender memories', but with a different purpose. Now in his thirties, and captivated by the new science of photography, Frith set out on a series of pioneering journeys to the Nile regions that occupied him from 1856 until 1860.

Intrigue and Adventure

He took with him on his travels a specially-designed wicker carriage that acted as both dark-room and sleeping chamber. These far-flung journeys were packed with intrigue and adventure. In his life story, written when he was sixty-three, Frith tells of being held captive by bandits, and of fighting 'an awful midnight battle to the very point of surrender with a deadly pack of hungry, wild dogs'. Sporting flowing Arab costume, Frith arrived at Akaba by camel seventy years before Lawrence, where he encountered 'desert princes and rival sheikhs, blazing with jewel-hilted swords'.

During these extraordinary adventures he was assiduously exploring the desert regions bordering the Nile and patiently recording the antiquities and peoples with his camera. He was the first photographer to venture beyond the sixth cataract. Africa was still the mysterious 'Dark Continent', and Stanley and Livingstone's historic meeting was a decade into the future. The conditions for picture taking confound belief. He laboured for hours in his wicker dark-room in the sweltering heat of the desert, while the volatile chemicals fizzed dangerously in their trays. Often he was forced to work in remote tombs and caves where conditions were cooler. Back in London he exhibited his photographs and was 'rapturously cheered' by members of the Royal Society. His reputation as a photographer was made overnight. An eminent modern historian has likened their impact on the population of the time to that on our own generation of the first photographs taken on the surface of the moon.

Venture of a Life-Time

Characteristically, Frith quickly spotted the opportunity to create a new business as a specialist publisher of photographs. He lived in an era of immense and sometimes violent change. For the poor in the early part of Victoria's reign work was a drudge and the hours long, and people had precious little free time to enjoy themselves. Most had no transport other than a cart or gig at their disposal, and had not travelled far beyond the

boundaries of their own town or village. However, by the 1870s, the railways had threaded their way across the country, and Bank Holidays and half-day Saturdays had been made obligatory by Act of Parliament. All of a sudden the ordinary working man and his family were able to enjoy days out and see a little more of the world.

With characteristic business acumen, Francis Frith foresaw that these new tourists would enjoy having souvenirs to commemorate their days out. In 1860 he married Mary Ann Rosling and set out with the intention of photographing every city, town and village in Britain. For the next thirty years he travelled the country by train and by pony and trap, producing fine photographs of seaside resorts and beauty spots that were keenly bought by millions of Victorians. These prints were painstakingly pasted into family albums and pored over during the dark nights of winter, rekindling precious memories of summer excursions.

The Rise of Frith & Co

Frith's studio was soon supplying retail shops all over the country. To meet the demand he gathered about him a small team of photographers, and published the work of independent artist-photographers of the calibre of Roger Fenton and Francis Bedford. In order to gain some understanding of the scale of Frith's business one only has to look at the catalogue issued by Frith & Co in 1886: it runs to some 670 pages, listing not only many thousands of views of the British Isles but also many photographs of most European countries, and China, Japan, the USA and

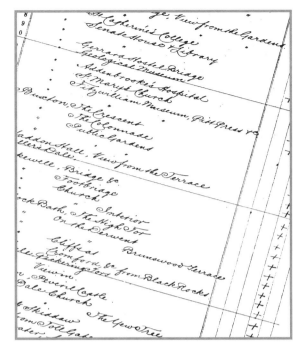

Canada – note the sample page shown above from the hand-written *Frith & Co* ledgers detailing pictures taken. By 1890 Frith had created the greatest specialist photographic publishing company in the world, with over 2,000 outlets – more than the combined number that Boots and WH Smith have today! The picture on the right shows the *Frith & Co* display board at Ingleton in the Yorkshire Dales. Beautifully constructed with mahogany frame and gilt inserts, it could display up to a dozen local scenes.

Postcard Bonanza

The ever-popular holiday postcard we know today took many years to develop. In 1870 the Post Office issued the first plain cards, with a pre-printed stamp on one face. In 1894 they allowed other publishers' cards to be sent through the mail with an attached adhesive halfpenny stamp. Demand grew rapidly, and in 1895 a new size of postcard was permitted called the court card, but there was little room for illustration. In 1899, a year after Frith's death, a new card measuring 5.5 x 3.5 inches became the standard format, but it was not until 1902 that the divided back came into being, with address and message on one face and a full-size illustration on the other. *Frith & Co* were in the vanguard of postcard development, and Frith's sons Eustace and Cyril continued their father's monumental task, expanding the number of views offered to the public and recording more and more places in Britain, as the coasts and countryside were opened up to mass travel.

Francis Frith died in 1898 at his villa in Cannes, his great project still growing. The archive he created continued in business for another seventy years. By 1970 it contained over a third of a million pictures of 7,000 cities, towns and villages. The massive photographic record Frith has left to us stands as a living monument to a special and very remarkable man.

Frith's Archive: *A Unique Legacy*

FRANCIS FRITH'S legacy to us today is of immense significance and value, for the magnificent archive of evocative photographs he created provides a unique record of change in 7,000 cities, towns and villages throughout Britain over a century and more. Frith and his fellow studio photographers revisited locations many times down the years to update their views, compiling for us an enthralling and colourful pageant of British life and character.

We tend to think of Frith's sepia views of Britain as nostalgic, for most of us use them to conjure up memories of places in our own lives with which we have family associations. It often makes us forget that to Francis Frith they were records of daily life as it was actually being lived in the cities, towns and villages of his day. The Victorian age was one of great and often bewildering change for ordinary people, and though the pictures evoke an impression of slower times, life was as busy and hectic as it is today.

We are fortunate that Frith was a photographer of the people, dedicated to recording the minutiae of everyday life. For it is this sheer wealth of visual data, the painstaking chronicle of changes in dress, transport, street layouts, buildings, housing, engineering and landscape that captivates us so much today. His remarkable images offer us a powerful link with the past and with the lives of our ancestors.

Today's Technology

Computers have now made it possible for Frith's many thousands of images to be accessed almost instantly. In the Frith archive today, each photograph is carefully 'digitised' then stored on a CD Rom. Frith archivists can locate a single photograph amongst thousands within seconds. Views can be catalogued and sorted under a variety of categories of place and content to the immediate benefit of researchers.

Inexpensive reference prints can be created for them at the touch of a mouse button, and a wide range of books and other printed materials assembled and published for a wider, more general readership - in the next twelve months over a hundred Frith local history titles will be published! The day-to-day workings of the archive are very different from how they were in Francis Frith's time: imagine the herculean task of sorting through eleven tons of glass negatives as Frith had to do to locate a particular

See Frith at www. frithbook.co.uk

sequence of pictures! Yet the archive still prides itself on maintaining the same high standards of excellence laid down by Francis Frith, including the painstaking cataloguing and indexing of every view.

It is curious to reflect on how the internet now allows researchers in America and elsewhere greater instant access to the archive than Frith himself ever enjoyed. Many thousands of individual views can be called up on screen within seconds on one of the Frith internet sites, enabling people living continents away to revisit the streets of their ancestral home town, or view places in Britain where they have enjoyed holidays. Many overseas researchers welcome the chance to view special theme selections, such as transport, sports, costume and ancient monuments.

We are certain that Francis Frith would have heartily approved of these modern developments in imaging techniques, for he himself was always working at the very limits of Victorian photographic technology.

The Value of the Archive Today

Because of the benefits brought by the computer, Frith's images are increasingly studied by social historians, by researchers into genealogy and ancestory, by architects, town planners, and by teachers and schoolchildren involved in local history projects.

In addition, the archive offers every one of us an opportunity to examine the places where we and our families have lived and worked down the years. Highly successful in Frith's own era, the archive is now, a century and more on, entering a new phase of popularity.

The Past in Tune with the Future

Historians consider the Francis Frith Collection to be of prime national importance. It is the only archive of its kind remaining in private ownership and has been valued at a million pounds. However, this figure is now rapidly increasing as digital technology enables more and more people around the world to enjoy its benefits.

Francis Frith's archive is now housed in an historic timber barn in the beautiful village of Teffont in Wiltshire. Its founder would not recognize the archive office as it is today. In place of the many thousands of dusty boxes containing glass plate negatives and an all-pervading odour of photographic chemicals, there are now ranks of computer screens. He would be amazed to watch his images travelling round the world at unimaginable speeds through network and internet lines.

The archive's future is both bright and exciting. Francis Frith, with his unshakeable belief in making photographs available to the greatest number of people, would undoubtedly approve of what is being done today with his lifetime's work. His photographs, depicting our shared past, are now bringing pleasure and enlightenment to millions around the world a century and more after his death.

Sheffield and the South

Sheffield has been famous since the 14th century for cutlery: it was Benjamin Huntsman's discovery that steel could be purified by using a crucible, that led to Sheffield becoming the steel capital of Britain. Forges, metal-working shops and steelworks came in all shapes and sizes, from those employing just a handful of men to the industrial giants like Firth Brown and Hadfields. There were other industries, such as the Yorkshire Engine Co. which built railway locomotives, and there were also several collieries within easy reach of the city centre. Badly damaged during the Second World War, much of the city centre was rebuilt; little now survives of the pre-Victorian era save for parts of the cathedral and a handful of houses.

Sheffield, Fitzalan Square 1902 48268
Electric street tramcars had been introduced in 1899; in this picture we have a selection of single-deckers and open-top double-deckers. The Corporation had taken over the tramway system in 1896, and lost no time in converting it from horse to electric traction. The single-deck trams were used on routes with low railway bridges. Note also the wooden stalls used as tramway stops.

Sheffield, The Canal Basin 1870 SI08001
Several barges are loaded with scrap metal en route for reprocessing. The canal came right into the heart of the city close to the Corn Exchange.

Sheffield, Fargate c1955 S108006
A tramcar trundles along Fargate. On the right is the Albany Hotel and the Yorkshire Penny Bank. Sheffield was just one of a handful of authorities at this date who still had faith in their tramway system. As late as 1948, the city was given a £200,000 loan from the Ministry of Transport to build 35 new trams.

Sheffield, Barkers Pool c1955 S108055

On the right is the Gaumont, a classic example of the super cinema of the 1930s. In those days many people went to the cinema at least once a week. These super cinemas were designed to take your mind of the drudgery of everyday life, so that for a few hours you could leave your worries behind and enter the world of make-believe.

Sheffield, Endcliffe Woods 1893 31976

This park was laid out for the benefit of working people to give them a break from the dust and grime of industrial Sheffield.

▼ Sheffield, Beauchief Abbey c1950 B335014
Beauchief Abbey lies four miles south of Sheffield. The abbey was founded in 1175; all that now remains is the west tower.

▼ Doncaster, The Parish Church 1903 49857
Here we see a Humber keel boat on the river. In the background is the great parish church of St George built in 1858 to replace an earlier one which had been destroyed by fire five years earlier. The story goes that as the old church went up in flames, the vicar exclaimed 'Good gracious, and I have left my false teeth in the vestry!'

▲ Doncaster, High Street 1895 35313
Along here could be found the imposing edifice of the York City & County Bank, the Yorkshire Penny Bank and the 18th-century Reindeer Hotel. Doncaster owes its transformation from an agricultural to an industrial centre to the coming of the railways. The Great Northern Railway chose Doncaster for the site of its locomotive and carriage and wagon workshops.

◄ Doncaster, Baxtergate 1903 49853

This is the junction of St Sepulchre Gate and the High Street. It was down Baxtergate that Freeman, Hardy and Willis had their branch. Coal mining was a major employer: Doncaster was ringed with pit villages. The first sod was cut at Brodsworth Colliery in 1905 and at Hatfield Main in 1911. At Hatfield it took five years to reach the Barnsley bed at 852 yards below the surface.

Conisbrough, The Castle 1895 35317A
The castle is set on a knoll overlooking the River Don. Built out of the local creamy-white limestone, the keep is 90 ft high and has six semi-hexagonal buttresses, which rise above it to form mini-turrets. When Sir Walter Scott visited Conisbrough, he was so impressed with the tiny chapel set into one of the buttresses that he included it in his novel 'Ivanhoe'.

Bradford & Industrial West Yorkshire

Without doubt Bradford was the centre of the woollen and worsted industry, not only in this country but throughout the world. The Victorian traveller would have found the city skyline a veritable forest of mill chimneys, but there were other industries. Bradford was on the western edge of the great Yorkshire coalfield, and because the coal was near to the surface, it could be mined relatively inexpensively. Also close by were the ironworks of Bowling and Low Moor.

Bradford, Market Street 1897 39509
In the background is the Venetian Gothic-style Wool Exchange, which was said to present an animated sight on Mondays and Thursdays when the traders did their buying and selling.

◀ **Bradford, Town Hall Square 1903** 49712
On the right is the Town Hall in all its Gothic splendour, which was completed in 1873 at a cost of £100,000.

◄ **Bradford, Tyrell Street 1903** 49713
Trams stop to pick up their passengers. Electric street tramcars were introduced in the city from 1898 and ran until 1950.

▼ **Bradford, Forster Square 1897** 39506
On the right is a statue of Richard Oastler, who fought against the use of child labour in the mills. The large building in the background is the Post Office, which was open from seven in the morning till ten at night.

◄ **Bradford, Victoria Square c1950** B173028
This view shows the square just before the abandonment of the tramway system. In the background a trolleybus is about to pass a tram as it heads towards the Town Hall. Like the electric tramcar, the trolleybus drew its power from overhead and did not require rails. In 1911, a joint scheme between Leeds and Bradford saw the inauguration of Britain's first trolleybus service.

Bradford, Forster Square 1903 49711
The square was named after the Bradford MP W E Forster, who sponsored the compulsory education act of 1870.
It was thanks to people like Forster that Bradford was the first to have school medical services, school meals, a
school board, school baths and nursery provision. Lurking behind the post office is the parish church, which
became a cathedral in 1919.

Bradford, Park Band Stand 1923 74400
The park is named after Lord Masham and includes a boating lake, a scented garden for the blind and the
Cartwright Memorial Hall, which was opened in 1904.

Halifax, The Town Hall 1900 H9001

Set in the foothills of the Pennines, Halifax is one of the great cloth towns of England and has been a producer of cloth since the 13th century. The Town Hall, in the background of this view, was designed in the Italian style by Sir Charles Barry in 1863, and is famous for its extraordinary-looking clock tower. Note also the rough pavement setts and the juddering cobbled road. On the left is a boy selling milk from the churn.

Halifax, Crown Street 1896 38778

On the left we have Smith's umbrella shop, which had just diversified into wedding and birthday presents. The Piece Hall, completed in 1779, was where wool merchants traded and weavers sold their pieces. This superb building still stands. It has 315 rooms on three stories around a quadrangle.

Halifax, Market Hall Entrance 1896 38777
Inside the market, stalls were laid out in regular rows, with clothing, material and footwear stalls to the middle and foodstuffs to the outside.

Halifax, General View c1965 H9068

St John's, which is the old parish church dating from the 12th century, is on the right-hand side almost surrounded by warehouses, factories and the railway. Halifax is also where English toffee was invented, and it was here in 1934 that Percy Shaw produced the first cats' eyes, or to give them their proper name, reflecting road studs.

Halifax, The Market Hall 1896 38782

The glass roof is supported on ornamental columns made of cast-iron. The market appears light and airy, and there seems to be plenty of space around the stalls.

Halifax, The Technical School 1896 38781
This photograph shows looms and other equipment installed in a workshop at the technical school; it shows the importance of the cloth industry to the town. Indeed, Halifax had been granted its own laws for dealing with people convicted of stealing cloth. The law was limited to the forest of Hardwick, including the 18 towns and villages within its boundary. Anyone found with stolen cloth 'shall be taken to the gibbet and there have his head cut from his body'. Halifax had a decapitating machine - Dr Guillotine simply improved on the idea.

◀ **Haworth, General View c1955** H194052
This grim hard-featured town of grey-stone houses became a place for textile factories. It was at Haworth parsonage that the three Bronte sisters, Charlotte, Emily and Anne lived and worked. Mr Bronte was the vicar of St Michael and All Angels. The church is still there, but the Brontes would only recognise the west tower, for the remainder was demolished and rebuilt in 1880.

Halifax, General View c1965

H9070

The railway cuts a swathe through Halifax, yet given the town's importance, there was a sense of outrage when the Manchester & Leeds Railway bypassed the town with no connecting branch line built. A branch line was promised as early as 1841, but until July 1844 the only way manufacturers could get their products to a rail-head was by horse and cart to Elland station.

Bingley, The Old Market House 1894

34755

Set in the valley of the River Aire, Bingley was once the classical picture of a 19th-century worsted-weaving and textile town, with its great mills and tall smokestacks. Note the stocks situated to the left of the base of the market cross.

Bingley, The River Aire 1923 74416

Over on the far side of the river, behind the brick wall, is part of the gasworks. When this picture was taken, the Aire had already been polluted for several decades, as mills discharged waste directly into it.

Saltaire, The Station 1909 61871
Saltaire is on the Midland Railway main line from Bradford to Skipton. Saltaire owes its existence to Sir Titus Salt, who moved his alpaca and mohair mills here in the 1850s. Sir Titus was convinced that his workers needed a healthier environment to live and work in.

Saltaire, The Park 1909 61872
Apart from the ladies with the perambulator, Saltaire Park appears to be deserted. It might have been a requirement that the Frith cameraman take the picture with as few people as possible in it. This was often done at this time, purely for commercial and not artistic reasons.

The Leeds and Liverpool Canal, Five-Rise Locks 1894 34748
The locks lifted boats and barges a full 60 ft, and is one of the most impressive groups of locks on the canal. The canal was a vital link for Bingley's manufacturers with the port of Liverpool.

Leeds, The Post Office and Revenue Office 1897 39088
Leeds was the industrial power house of the old West Riding. There was an enormous variety to the manufacturing base of the city, including railway locomotives from the Hunslet Engine Co., Manning Wardle & Co., Kitsons, and Hudswell Clarke. The postal service in Victorian times was considered a vital part of the public good with offices in major cities having long opening hours.

Leeds, The Parish Church of St Peter, Kirkgate 1891 28281
There are no medieval churches in central Leeds, though several date from the 17th and 18th centuries. John Fowler & Co. built roadrollers, traction engines and farm machinery, and there were a number of companies producing castings of various sorts. There were bleaching works, flax mills, leather factories and chemical plants. Leeds also became the leading centre for the manufacture of ready-to-wear clothes.

Leeds, The Yorkshire College 1894 34767
It was out of this college that Leeds university was established in 1904. Leeds Mechanics' Institute was also noted for its high standards. Members of the Institute were also adventurous, hiring Thomas Cook in June 1840 to organise a members' excursion to York by way of the Leeds & Selby and the York & North Midland Railways. The trip was priced at half the normal fare and included tea at York.

Leeds, Headingley 1897 39099
The home of Yorkshire CCC.

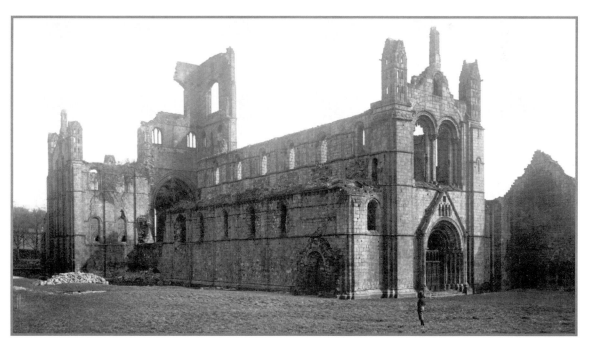

Leeds, Kirkstall Abbey 1891 28286
The abbey played a part in the industrial development of Leeds, for it was here that iron forging first began in the district. The Abbey was founded in 1152 as a daughter house of Fountains. Building work was completed by 1175, and iron forging began in 1200.

Ilkley, Skipton & The Moors

Ilkley was just another one-horse town until 1850; then the spring waters were declared beneficial to health, and so another spa town was born. Villas, hotels and hydros sprang up, and within a few years Ilkley was claiming to be the Malvern of the North.

Ilkley, Brook Street 1911 63557
Carriages wait patiently on the station approach for another train-load of health-seekers bound for any of the seven listed hydros. Taking the treatment cost £2.5s.0d a week, though a number of guides hinted that the local bracing air had perhaps as much medicinal value as the waters.

▼ **Ilkley, The Grove 1911** 63556

The road to the right leads to the railway station, but directly along the leafy street is The Spa, a particularly popular hydro.

▼ **Ilkley, The Open Air Bathing Pool c1960** 16006

There was a time when most places seemed to possess an open air pool, and though popular on hot sunny days, many were in fact closed down for various health and safety reasons.

▲ **Bolton Abbey c1886**
18510
The ruins of Bolton Abbey are near a sweeping bend of the River Wharfe, and proved a great attraction for painters, including Landseer and Turner. The priory was founded in the 12th century, and building work continued right up to the Dissolution. The nave survived, to be used as the parish church; during the late 19th century the rectory served as a free school.

◀ Ilkley, The Moors 1914
67335

At the time when this picture was taken, moorland walking had still to catch on; most walkers were ill-equipped, and ladies were expected to turn out in long dresses and totally inadequate footwear. One popular walk was up Heber's Gill to the Swastika Stone, an ancient area which may have been used for fire worship.

Skipton, High Street 1893 33157
Skipton was a centre for sheep and cattle rearing, as we can see from this busy market day scene. Situated at the edge of a wild tract of limestone country, the town was generally called Skipton-in-Craven. Its two main features are the castle, which withstood a three-year siege from December 1642 to December 1645, and the extensively restored Holy Trinity Church, which can be seen in the background. It was damaged during the siege of the castle in the Civil War. It contains some elaborate monuments to the Clifford Family, and was restored by Lady Anne Clifford before she died in 1675.

Skipton, Swadford Street 1923 74507
By this date the motorcar and charabanc had put Skipton firmly on the map as the principal southern gateway to the Dales. The town boasted one RAC-listed and two AA-recommended hotels, namely The Ship, The Black Horse and The Devonshire.

Grassington, The Market Square 1900 45779
The village had once been a centre for lead-mining, but now relied on agriculture and quarrying. In 1902 the railway finally came to Grassington with the opening of a line to Skipton.

Burnsall, On the River 1900 45794
In the background is St Wilfred's, which was repaired in 1612 at the expense of Sir William Craven. The church houses an 11th-century font and some fragments of Anglo-Saxon sculpture. At the oar of the boat is a woman - quite adventurous for 1900.

Clapham, The Upper Falls 1900 45769
In 1857, Ingleborough Cave was made accessible; thereafter, Clapham became a centre for potholing. Nearby is
Gaping Gill, which has an underground chamber large enough to house a cathedral.

Ingleton, The Village 1890 26330
Ingleton is set amid the spectacular scenery of the River Greta and Clapham Beck. Francis Frith had already set up a stockist to sell his postcards; the display board is to the left of the shop window.

Settle, The Market 1921 71339
Here we see the bustling Tuesday market. On the right is the Elizabethan-style Town Hall built in 1832. In the background, smothered with drying washing, are the shambles. These date from the 17th century, and comprised several shops in an arched arcade with living accommodation above.

Harrogate Around & About

Harrogate is one of the oldest and most favourite of all the English spa towns. The curative mineral springs were discovered here by Sir William Slingsby in 1571. In the 1840s the town was developed by the Duchy of Lancaster, and the first public baths opened in 1842.

Harrogate, Valley Gardens 1907 58645
This was a favourite venue for mild constitutionals after taking the waters. Here a small crowd no doubt enjoy an afternoon concert party given by a Pierrot troupe.

▼ **Harrogate, Crescent Gardens 1911** 63514

Two elegantly dressed ladies take an afternoon stroll. In the background the crowd is gathering, and the awnings are being taken down off the bandstand. The music is about to begin.

▼ **Harrogate, The Royal Pump Room 1923** 74569

In 1902, bumpers of sulphuric and chalybeate were dispensed here from seven o'clock in the morning onwards. After taking the first glass, a mild constitutional in Valley Gardens was recommended.

▲ **Harrogate, Parliament Street 1907** 58649

Sign wars! On the right, Taylor' Drug Store boldly displays its name in six foot high gilt lettering. Not to be outdone, the chemist just across the road proclaims that his establishment is the largest in the world. Harrogate had become a fashionable town noted for its fine shops and rich teas.

◄ Harrogate, The New Baths 1897 39430
This view was taken shortly after the Royal Baths opened. They were said to be unequalled in decoration and roominess, and for 5/6d you could get a mud bath with electricity. From 1949, the cure was available on the NHS.

Ripley, The Village 1923 74585

When this picture was taken, Ripley consisted of just one street. The village was extensively remodelled in the 1820s, though parts of the parish church date from the 14th century. This picture shows the cobbled square, complete with stocks and the village cross. In the churchyard is what is claimed to be the only weeping cross in the whole of Yorkshire. Around the base are eight niches in which to kneel and repent.

Ripon, The Cathedral 1895 35260

Ripon is one of England's smallest cathedral cities; in 1836 it became the centre of a new bishopric. The cathedral looks massive, but is in fact relatively small; the central and two western towers are of no great height. The original church built by St Wilfred was destroyed in 950 AD. The present cathedral dates from the 12th and 13th centuries; the west front is one of the finest examples of Early English work still extant.

Ripon, Market Place 1901 47179
The obelisk dates from 1781 and was raised to commemorate William Aislabie, who was the local MP for sixty years.

Fountains Abbey 1895 35278
Founded in poverty in 1132 by a group of monks from St Mary's Abbey, York, Fountains eventually became very wealthy. The ruins date from the 12th to the 15th centuries; the tower, which was built between 1492 and 1524, is the latest part.

**Fountains Abbey
1886** 18352
Henry VIII sold
Fountains to Sir Richard
Gresham in 1540, and
though some seventy
years later Sir Stephen
Proctor used abbey
stone to build Fountains
Hall, the ruins are still
impressive and
preserve the plan of
this great monastery
almost intact.

◄ **Thirsk, Market Day c1955** T306030
During the 18th and 19th centuries, Thirsk was one of the posting stations serving the Great North Road; The Fleece was the main coaching inn.

◄ Aldborough, The Village 1907 58636

Aldborough, just one mile from Boroughbridge, stands on the site of the Roman station Isurium, and has a museum containing Roman remains. In this picture, children play round the old stone cross, said to commemorate the Battle of Boroughbridge. The carter has stopped to let the cameraman take the picture. Note that the girls all appear to be wearing smocks and hats.

▼ Boroughbridge, The Three Greyhounds Hotel 1907 58630

Boroughbridge dates back to Norman times, when a bridge was constructed over the River Ure. In 1322 the Earl of Lancaster sought refuge in the local church following his defeat by Edward II. The unfortunate earl was taken prisoner and carted off to his own castle at Pontefract, where he was beheaded. Boroughbridge probably saw its best days when it was a coaching town for traffic on the Great North Road, and had no less than twenty-two inns.

◄ Knaresborough, Market Day 1921 71687

The ancient market town of Knaresborough clings to the limestone bluff of a gorge carved by the River Nidd, and is famous for several things: the oldest woollen mill in England, Mother Shipton, a 15th-century prophetess who allegedly forecast motorcars and aircraft, and Blind Jack Metcalf, born in 1717, who was a soldier, roadbuilder, forest guide and musician.

Knaresborough, Town and River 1888
20946
The church on the left is St John's, the tower of which is topped off with a small spirelet and dates from the 13th and 14th centuries. In 1318, a Scottish raiding party attempted to destroy the tower and the people who had taken shelter there by setting it alight. The Scots failed, but for centuries afterwards traces of the burning could still be seen.

Knaresborough, Ferry to the Dropping Well 1911 63532
Moored alongside the far bank is a floating tea room which appears to be doing a brisk trade. The rowing boat in the foreground is in fact the ferry to the Dropping Well. On the hill above the town stand the ruins of Knaresborough Castle, which was destroyed by Parliament in 1648.

Knaresborough, 'Mother Shipton' Inn 1914 67264
This is a petrifying well, similar to the one at Matlock Bath in Derbyshire, where the limestone content of the spring water solidifies objects which fall into it. At one time there was a petrified mongoose on exhibition!

Knaresborough, The Castle 1906 55009
A Norman castle had been built here by Baron Serlo de Burg, but the ruins date from the 14th century. During the reign of King John, the castle was a royal arsenal, manufacturing 109,000 crossbow quarrels. In the early years of Edward II's reign, Knaresborough was extensively rebuilt owing to the lordship having been given to the king's favourite, Piers Gaveston. It was also here that Richard II was imprisoned, prior to being taken to Pontefract where he was murdered.

Wetherby, The High Street 1909 61730
The Angel Hotel on the left was one of three to cater for the motorist; the others were the George and Dragon and the Brunswick. Wetherby had been an important stopover during the days of the stagecoach, but since the coming of the railways it has had to rely more and more on tourists.

◀ **Wetherby, The Market Place 1909** 61729
At the turn of the century Wetherby was described as 'a town with no interest'. In 1920 the Dunlop Guide added 'pleasant walks along the river'.

Wetherby, North Street 1909 61731

Ward & Sons were established in 1868, and had probably been smiths and/or farriers, until deciding to concentrate on vehicle repairs and the selling of bicycles. As can be seen from the picture, they were also the local AA agents. Further down the street Continental Motors are the local Michelin agents.

Boston Spa, Street Scene 1893 32000

In 1744 a man by the name of John Shires discovered a saline spring, and thanks to the 18th-century fashion for taking the waters Boston Spa was born. Like most spas, Boston had its moment of glory, and for a few years was the place to seen. A stagecoach service operated on a daily basis from Leeds and back, and wealthy travellers using the Great North Road would stop over and sample the delights of the pump room.

Clifford, the Village 1897 39445

This village is just one mile from Boston Spa and even less from the Great North Road. One of the interesting things when looking at some of these photographs is the number of shops that even the smallest of villages seemed to have. Nowadays, we have been sucked in to thinking that convenience shopping is something wonderful, village shops, post offices, and even pubs are in decline.

The Yorkshire Coast

Hull, the third largest port in Britain, still has docks running for several miles along the north bank of the Humber, handling hundreds of millions of pounds worth of cargo and thousands of passengers every year. And despite savage reductions in the fishing fleet and the EU quota system, it remains one of our principal fishing ports, though much of the fish is either landed from foreign trawlers or arrives by lorry from other UK ports. The pictures from the Frith collection were mostly taken in the early 20th century, when Hull made its living almost exclusively from the sea and shipbuilding. The pictures are also of interest because Hull was virtually rebuilt after the Second World War, having been the hardest hit of all the northern ports.

Hull, The Market Place 1903 49809
To the right is the Cross Keys Hotel, but the most famous of all is Ye Old White Harte Inn, where the Governor and other leading citizens of Hull took the decision not to let King Charles I enter the city in 1642.

Hull, The Market Place 1903 49813
The ancient parish church of Holy Trinity dates from the 13th to the 15th centuries and has an unusual brick-built chancel.

Hull, George Street 1903 49814
Here we see an open-top tramcar; electric trams had been introduced to the city in 1899. On 30 June 1945, Hull became the first city in the country to abandon its tramway since the outbreak of the Second World War. Many of the trams were sold to the Leeds Corporation.

Hull, The Dock Offices 1903 49807
These imposing Dock Offices reinforce Hull's position as a major port. The Doric column on the right is a monument to William Wilberforce, who was born in Hull, and was responsible for the abolition of slavery throughout the Empire.

Hull, The Humber 1903 49820
As well as general cargo shipped through the port, the amount of fish landed at St Andrew's Dock during this year, amounted to 1,580,959 cwts.

▼ **Bridlington, Princess Street 1897** 39371

Bridlington lies near the top of Bridlington Bay, its northern flank protected by the great headland of Flamborough some six miles distant. The old town is in fact one mile inland from the sea, where in 1119, Walter de Grant founded an Augustinian priory. This view shows one of the principal shopping streets for this town of around 13,000 people. During the holiday season, the town's population could easily double - Bridlington was within easy reach of trippers from Hull, Leeds, Beverley and York.

▼ **Filey, Looking South toward Flamborough Head 1901** 48020A

Deckchairs and beach tents were available for hire, and the donkeys are saddled to take different age groups. The harp and the clown-like costumes are in fact the tell-tale signs that a Pierrot seaside concert party is touting for customers. Pierrot were in vogue right up to the Second World War, and their origins go back to the London success of the mime play 'L'Enfant Prodigue' staged in 1891.

▲ **Bridlington, Princess Parade 1906** 55752

This view shows some of the well-laid-out flower-beds that Bridlington had a reputation for producing. A significant date in Bridlington's history was 22 February 1643, when Queen Henrietta Maria landed at Bridlington with much-needed arms and ammunition for King Charles. Bombarded by warships of the Parliamentary navy, the Queen took shelter until it was considered safe to move on to Boynton Hall.

◀ **Filey, The Promenade 1897** 39343
On the right, Archibald Ramsden's bathing machines offer discreet changing facilities. The small horse-drawn carts carried less active holiday-makers onto the sands, but could probably be hired as an alternative to a donkey ride. Situated eleven miles north of Bridlington, Filey was for many years a working fishing village, but became a popular place in the 1890s for those seeking a quiet holiday.

Scarborough, Westborough 1891
28817
An ancient town as well as a seaport, Scarborough takes its name from the cliffs or scars surrounding it. Westborough is one of the main thoroughfares linking the North Eastern Railway station and the town. On the right is Winebloom's Railway Hotel and Robinson's Cash Boot Stores, whilst over on the left is Graham's Adelphi Commercial Hotel.

Scarborough, Belmont 1890 23476
Here a group of people take the chance to admire the view over Spa Cliffs, or catch up with the latest news. The Spa by this time was long gone, having been destroyed by fire in 1876. In its place an exotic Turkish-style pavilion was built containing a concert hall, art gallery, theatre and restaurant.

◀ **Scarborough, The South Cliff Tramway 1890** 23459
The tramway offered holiday-makers an alternative means of escape from the beach to the Esplanade, other than by the 224 steps cutting through the Spa Gardens, and all for just 1d. At just under 21 miles from Whitby, Scarborough rapidly developed to become the premier resort of the Yorkshire coast, and was often overrun with day trippers, as Blackpool was.

◄ Scarborough, The Spa Promenade 1890 23453

On the beach in the background are a number of bathing machines. Ladies wishing to bathe would enter the machines from the landward side and horses would haul the contraptions down into the water. Meanwhile, the ladies were donning their bathing apparel inside, and would emerge through the door and slip, dignity intact, into the shallows. Whilst they were bathing, the horses would be harnessed to the other end of the machines for the return journey.

▼ Scarborough, Foreshore Road 1891 28812

Scarborough Castle, on the skyline, once stood 100 ft tall, with walls 12 ft thick; the keep was positioned in such a way so as to command the approach to the causeway leading to the castle. Any attacking force attempting to enter the bailey would first of all have to run the gauntlet of defending fire from the keep's battlements. Scarborough endured two determined sieges in 1645 and 1648; on both occasions the garrison surrendered to the Roundheads.

◄ Scarborough, Foreshore Road 1890 23464

This view looks away from the castle. In the foreground is a market where trippers could buy fresh fish off the local boats. On the right is the lifeboat station. The lifeboat was slung on a wheeled cradle which would be hauled out of the station, down the ramp immediately in front of it, and into the sea; the boat floated off once there was sufficient water under her.

Scarborough, Vincents Pier 1890 23471
The paddle steamer 'Comet' loads up with passengers for an excursion trip round the headland. These small steamers were a feature of both the Scarborough and Bridlington holiday trade; they survived until they were replaced by screw vessels in the 1930s.

Scarborough, The Harbour 1890 23466
A Lowestoft-registered fishing boat slips out to sea unnoticed by the anglers on the harbour. In the background is the imposing, if somewhat overpowering, edifice of the Grand Hotel. By 1920 Scarborough could boast no less than ten top hotels, including the 100-bedroom Pavilion and the 160-bedroom Manor Private. The telephone number for the Grand was Scarborough 11.

Robin Hood's Bay, The Bay Hotel 1927 80187
The fishing village of Robin Hood's Bay lies just a few miles to the south of Whitby. Also known as Bay Town, the village became a favourite haunt for artists and holidaymakers alike. The connection with the legend of Robin Hood is obscure, but one story is that Robin came here to hire boats in order to escape from England. For decades, just as in this picture, people have sunned themselves along the sea wall. The Bay Hotel is on the right.

Robin Hood's Bay, General View 1927 80183
Part of the village is clustered around the top of a ravine; notice the steep flight of steps in the lower foreground dropping away down toward the sea. In the background, the bay sweeps round to Ravenscar, the 'town that never was'. Apparently there were plans to turn Ravenscar into another Scarborough, but the scheme failed owing to the unstable geology of the area.

Robin Hood's Bay, On the Beach 1927 80185
One of the reasons why Robin Hood's Bay proved to be a popular haunt for artists is the picturesque cluster of red-roofed cottages perched somewhat precariously on the cliffs. Over the last 200 years or so, erosion has only managed to claim two rows of houses and a road.

Whitby, The Abbey 1901 46790
It was here in the 7th century that St Hilda founded one of the most famous monasteries of the Celtic world. Here worked Caedmon, the first recorded English Christian poet. The ruins are of the abbey that replaced the first one in the 13th century. Adjacent to the Abbey is the parish church of St Mary's, which is reached from the harbour by a flight of 199 steps known as 'Jacob's Ladder'. St Mary's was made famous in Bram Stoker's novel 'Dracula'.

Whitby, The Bridge 1913 66266
The bridge was a favourite place where people could stop for a chat, or simply stand and watch the world go by. The small hut is the control point for the bridge, which could be raised to allow shipping through.

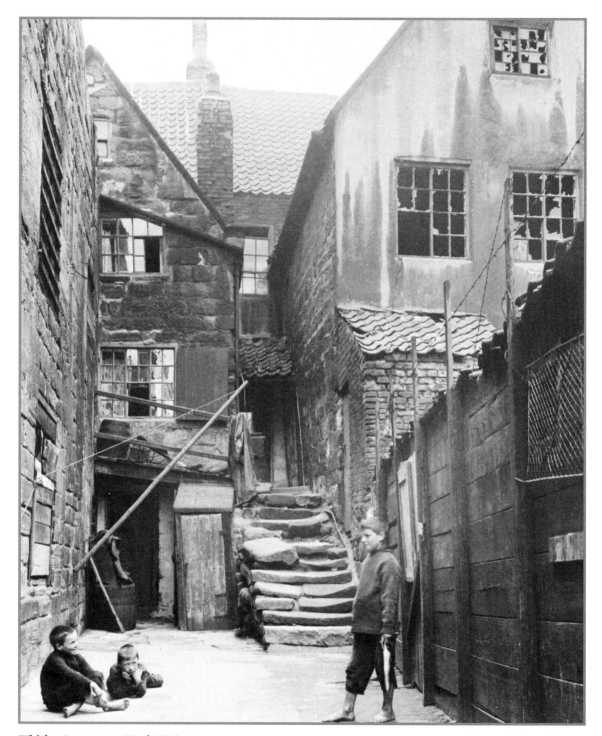

Whitby, Arguments Yard 1913 66290

Situated in a deep ravine on the estuary of the river Esk, Whitby earned its living from the sea, either by whaling, fishing, coastal trading or shipbuilding. For centuries it was often easier for people coming to or going from Whitby to make their journey by sea rather than attempt to travel overland. Here, in Arguments Yard, the house on the right is derelict, the stone stairs have seen better days and the outside toilet looks ready to collapse.

Whitby, Baxtergate 1923 74309
In the centre of town, Baxtergate contained the post office, The Angel Hotel (telephone number Whitby 57) and St John's Church, as well as many shops. By this time, Whitby could boast no less than five hotels in the Dunlop Motorist's Guide, The Angel, The Royal (with 172 bedrooms and garage parking for 20 cars), The Metropole, The Custom House and the 70-bedroom West Cliff.

Whitby, St Anne's Staith 1886 18167
The coming of the railway changed Whitby. It was now firmly on the map: its narrow crowded alleys and harbourside streets, its ruined abbey and its souvenirs made from jet, fossilised wood found in the local area, proved a magnet for day trippers and holiday-makers. The holiday trade led to the development of the town, chiefly in the direction of the West Cliff, where hotels and guest houses were built.

Sandsend, The Beach 1925 78993
Sandsend was just three miles along the sandy beach from Whitby. It was a popular place for holidays when this picture was taken, even though the village was disfigured by a ruin of an alum works and an iron bridge carrying the LNER railway line from Whitby to Saltburn. To the north lies the Kettleness, or rather what is left of it. During a violent storm in 1829, the cliff fell into the sea taking most of Kettleness with it.

Runswick Bay, The Village 1886 18202

The fishing village of Runswick Bay is set on a sheer cliff. It is also one of the most attractive harbourless villages along the Yorkshire coast. When this picture was taken, fishermen would have to wait for high tide before launching their boats from the beach.

Runswick Bay, The Shore 1927 80194

Even when they were not fishing, fishermen always had work to do, repairing nets and maintaining the boats. Perhaps the fisherman is yarning to the children about the hob (a Yorkshire goblin) who is said to live in the hollows to the south of the village. The hob was fond of children, and was able to cure ailments.

Staithes, The Village 1925 79004
During the 19th and early 20th centuries, Staithes was a fishing port of some standing, a centre for cod, haddock and mackerel, but it fell into decline with the development of steam trawlers, which tended to be concentrated on the larger ports. At one time the North Eastern Railway ran three or four special fish trains a week out of Staithes. As with other fishing villages along the Yorkshire coast, Staithes clings to the sides of steep cliffs and ravines. Though the old gentleman could well be delivering fresh milk, yokes were used for carrying all sorts of things up the steep streets.

Staithes, The Bridge 1886 18208
The village is said to have begun as a result of a shipwreck, when the survivors from a French ship scrambled ashore and decided to stay. As with Robin Hood's Bay, smuggling was a way of life here in the 18th century. Lining was one of the principal methods of catching fish. These are fairly small lines for use by local fishermen; trawlers, however, would tow a line perhaps half a mile or more in length, which with branches could have as many as 15,000 hooks.

Swaledale

Swaledale lies to the north of Wensleydale; its main industry during the 18th and 19th centuries was lead mining. One of the principal centres was at Reeth, the largest community in Swaledale apart from Richmond, which by 1823 had a population of over 1400. By the 1880s, competition from overseas suppliers sounded the death knell for the lead mining industry, and Swaledale reverted to farming.

Richmond, The Castle and the Bridge 1923
74350
The town of Richmond grew up round the Norman castle, which was begun around the year 1071 by Alan Rufus, a son of the Duke of Brittany, and William the Conqueror's man in these parts. The Norman fortress dominates the entrance to Swaledale. When the castle was begun, the border between that part of England firmly under Norman control and those still willing to put up a fight lay just a few miles to the north.

Richmond, The Castle Keep 1909 59493
A steep lane climbs up round the edge of the castle. This picture gives us an idea of the impressive appearance of
the 12th-century keep. Richmond is one of those castles where the keep is positioned at or near the gate, which
suggests that it was intended for an offensive, rather than defensive role. It also contains Scollard's Hall, built in
1080 and probably the oldest domestic building in Britain.

Richmond, The Market Place 1908 59492
By the time the castle was finished in around 1200, Richmond had grown in size; a market has been held here since 1155. By 1440 the town was trading in dairy produce, wine, fish, garlic, silk, iron, coal, copper and lead. In the background is Holy Trinity Church, a most unusual building, which in the 1900s included a tobacconist, a bank, and two butchers' shops as component parts. It now houses the regimental museum of The Green Howards.

Muker, The Village 1896 38295
The village of Muker, set toward the western end of the dale, dates back to 1274. After a chapel of ease was built here in 1580, the delightfully named Corpse Way gradually fell into disuse. Until then, the bodies of people from Upper Swaledale had to be carried all the way to Grinton Church for Christian burial. Along the route there were coffin stones, on which the coffin was placed whilst the bearers got their breath back. Apparently one of these stones still exists and can be seen on the north side of Ivelet Bridge.

Easby, The Abbey 1893 32290
Here we see the remains of the Premonstratensian Abbey of St Agatha. The abbey was founded in 1155 by the Constable of Richmond Castle; the members of the Order were known as the White Canons after the colour of their habits.

Hipswell Hall 1913 66034
Close to what would become Catterick Camp, Hipswell Hall had seen better days than when this picture was taken.
When the camp was built, it took in Scotton Hall, the Hipswell estate and the Brough estate.

Catterick, The Village 1913 65487
It was at Catterick in AD 625 that Paulinus, first Bishop of York, baptised converts to Christianity, following the
marriage of King Edwin of Northumbria to Ethelburga of Kent. Catterick is the site of the Roman city of
Catteractonium.

Wensleydale

Granted a market charter by William III, Hawes later became a centre for textiles, quarrying and the production of Wensleydale cheese. The town's growth was helped with the coming of the railways. Cheese production had been farmhouse-based, but towards the end of the last century a factory was built.

Hawes, The School 1900 45635
Behind and to the right is the turreted tower of the parish church. Built in 1851, it replaced the original church dating from the reign of Richard III.

◀ **Bainbridge, The Green 1906** 56025
It is believed that Bainbridge was a settlement for woodsmen working in the great forest of Wensleydale. An annual custom associated with this tradition is the blowing of a forest horn every night from the end of September to Shrovetide.

Bainbridge, The Village 1924 75709

Bainbridge was once an important junction, for here the roads to and from Lancaster, Swaledale and Westmorland met. In Roman times a fort stood on nearby Brough Hill, and a garrison was maintained here from about AD 80 to around the end of the 4th century. The old arched bridge crosses the Bain, which at just 6 miles in length is reputed to be the shortest river in England.

Addleborough, Farm Workers 1914 67235

Addleborough peak is in the background; it is believed to be named after a British chieftain, Authulf.

Askrigg, The Old Market Cross 1911 63468

Askrigg was already prosperous when the Domesday book was compiled, and continued as the commercial and industrial centre of Upper Wensleydale until 1699, when Hawes was granted a market charter. Many of the people who worked in the mills or mines lived in dilapidated cottages hidden behind the imposing three-storey buildings on the main street.

Askrigg, Main Street 1914 67231
One of Askrigg's main industries was clockmaking, and it is said that more timepieces were made here than anywhere else in the North Riding. Other local industries included brewing, spinning, dyeing, cotton and worsted manufacture and lead mining.

Aysgarth, The Village 1908 60790
Lying about ten miles east of Hawes, Aysgarth is famous for a series of waterfalls on the River Ure, the upper of which can still be viewed from a 16th-century single-arch bridge. The village became popular with visitors to the falls.

Castle Bolton, The Village 1911 63473

In the background are the ruins of Bolton Castle, which was built by Richard Scrope in the 1380s. Though designed as a fortress, the castle's principal function appears to have been residential; it was one of the first to have chimneys. Mary Queen of Scots was imprisoned here for six months, and the castle was partially dismantled at the end of the Civil War. The castle was then used by local families who lived in tenements built within the walls; the last of these left in 1898.

Leyburn, The Market Place from the Church Tower 1889 21690

Once nothing more than a tiny hamlet in the parish of Wensley, Leyburn developed into a market town thanks to a charter granted by Charles I. The church appears to be about six hundred years old, but was in fact only built in 1836; until then Leyburn had no church.

Leyburn, Market Place 1914 67223
Unlike Hawes and Askrigg, Leyburn never became industrialised, but it did become a fashionable place to retire to, doubling its population during the early years of Victoria's reign. For some years it boasted a theatre, and the Leyburn Shawl Tea Festivals attracted thousands of visitors The building on the left is the Bolton Arms Hotel. A fine Georgian building, the hotel came complete with a Long Room where Leyburn Market Club, founded in 1832, still holds its dinners. In the market place is an iron ring said to date back to the days of bull-baiting.

▼ **Middleham, The Market Place 1896** 38270
Middleham was once a major market town, but it is famous for two things: the training of racehorses, and its castle, home to Richard III. It passed into the hands of the Neville family, and Richard came here to be tutored by the Earl of Warwick, whose daughter Anne he later married. The author Charles Kingsley was an honorary canon at the church of St Alkelda and St Mary.

▼ **Bedale, St Gregory's Church 1896** 38280
The church was restored in 1854, though the tower itself dates from the 14th and 15th centuries. There is a room on the first floor, reached by a stair and guarded by a portcullis, which suggests that this was a defensive position for use when the Scots came on one of their cattle raids. The Scots are known to have raided at least as far south as Bradford.

▲ **Bedale, From the Tower of St Gregory's Church 1896** 38283
In the centre is the old cross: the blur to the left is a pony and trap moving too quickly for the photographer's camera. The market town of Bedale is just a few miles to the north-east of Masham. With its cobbled main street, wide square and bustling market, Bedale sits astride a long, low hill on the edge of Wensleydale.

◄ **Masham, Silver Street 1908** 60706
Masham straddles the River Ure. One of Masham's distinctive features is its large market place, where fairs would see as many as 70,000 to 80,000 sheep and lambs up for sale. Masham's claim to fame is that it is the home of Theakstons, brewers since 1827. The Bay Horse Inn was one of several hostelries serving the needs of visitors and locals alike.

York & the Vale of York

The walled city of York was for centuries the second most important city in England. Fortified by the Romans, it was here in AD 306 that Constantine the Great was proclaimed emperor. The historical and cultural capital of northern England, York has managed to survive the ravages of time, and is still able to offer visitors a fascinating glimpse into its 2000 years of history.

York, Bootham Bar 1911 63585
Note the overhead wires for the trams. York was a late comer to electric trams: the system did not open until January 1910, and even then it only lasted 25 years.

◀ **York, Goodramgate 1892** 30631
The Victorians loved York, and before the railway came, travellers could get here either by stage or mail-coach; there was also a steamboat service to and from London. The opening to the left of Todds leads to College Street and St William's College. The shops to the left were demolished in 1902-3 to make way for Deangate.

York, Low Petergate
1892 30632

On the right is Merriman's pawnbrokers with its ornate gas lamp, whilst on the left is Seale's brush and mat warehouse. Note the large broomhead, which is now in the Castle Museum, hanging over the shop.

York, Stonegate 1892
30633

Most of the stone used in the construction of the Minster was carried up this street. The names of streets and alleys are sometimes strange, such as Whipmawhopmagate and Jubbergate. One of the more interesting was Mucky Peg's Lane, which unfortunately was changed to Finkle Street.

York, The Minster
1908 59785

The coming of the railways put York firmly on the tourist map. Though the lines were owned by the North Eastern, no less than five other companies had running powers into the city. For decades, the first indication for those travelling by train that York was just a few miles away was the sight of the lofty towers of the Minster rising majestically above the city.

**York, Coney Street
1909** 61723
This is a fashionable
place for shopping -
note the liveried
coachman and the
motorcar. Bicycles
appear to be a popular
mode of transport for
the ladies.

York, The Shambles 1909 61722
The shelves at the front of the shops and the hooks overhead indicate that these were butchers' shops.

York, Lendal Bridge 1909 61702
Built of cast-iron, the bridge was opened in 1863 and improved the city by giving direct access to the original railway station, which was situated within the city walls.

York, View from the City Walls 1897 39492
This view looks towards Lendal Bridge and the towering bulk of the Minster. The road at the right leads to the original railway station, whilst the road cutting under the city wall leads to the new station built in the 1870s.

York, Barges on the Ouse 1886 18494
For centuries the Ouse had been used to transport people and goods in and out of the city. In the mid-1830s there was even a steamer service linking York with London. The journey took over thirty hours, and was an acceptable alternative to being shaken and bounced along the Great North Road in a mail-coach.

York, the Old Rectory 1910 61864
A medieval jettied building with soaring roof and Georgian windows, this old Rectory had been converted into a shop. Street gaslighting was introduced into the city in March 1824, replacing earlier oil lamps.

Tadcaster, The Market Place and Kirkgate 1907 58627
Nine miles from York on the road to Leeds, Tadcaster was once the Roman outpost of Calcaria. Two miles to the south is the hamlet of Towton, where on 29 March 1461 a bloody battle involving an estimated 50,000 troops took place. This picture was taken from the junction with Bridge Street. Just getting into the picture on the right is the recently completed Becketts Bank.

Tadcaster, The Mill on the Wharfe 1906 54852
Since the 18th century, the town has been a centre for the brewing of beer. The breweries used the Wharfe to bring in raw materials and transport finished products. But the river was prone to flooding, with the result that between 1875 and 1877 St Mary's Church was dismantled, moved, and then re-erected out of reach of the waters. In the background is the early 18th-century Wharfe Bridge.

Selby, The Toll-Bridge 1918 68170

The wooden toll-bridge over the Ouse was built in the 18th century. Selby still sees small ships loading and unloading at the modest wharf. Shipbuilding was also carried on here, the yard specialising in fishing vessels, tugboats and inland waterways craft. Because of the width of the river, vessels were launched sideways. In the background is the abbey church, dating from around 1100.

Selby, The Market Place and the Abbey 1913 65561

The abbey was founded by Benedict of Auxerre, who was instructed in a vision to go to Selebaie in England. Armed with one of the fingers from St Germain, Benedict set off. As he sailed up the Ouse, three swans settled in the water where Selby now stands. Taking this for a sign, Benedict planted a cross, built a hut, and with a lot of help from King William the abbey was founded.

Index

Frith Book Co Titles

Frith Book Company publish over a 100 new titles each year. For latest catalogue please contact Frith Book Co.

Town Books 96pp, 100 photos. County and Themed Books 128pp, 150 photos (unless specified) All titles hardback laminated case and jacket except those indicated pb (paperback)

Around Barnstaple	1-85937-084-5	£12.99
Around Blackpool	1-85937-049-7	£12.99
Around Bognor Regis	1-85937-055-1	£12.99
Around Bristol	1-85937-050-0	£12.99
Around Cambridge	1-85937-092-6	£12.99
Cheshire	1-85937-045-4	£14.99
Around Chester	1-85937-090-X	£12.99
Around Chesterfield	1-85937-071-3	£12.99
Around Chichester	1-85937-089-6	£12.99
Cornwall	1-85937-054-3	£14.99
Cotswolds	1-85937-099-3	£14.99
Around Derby	1-85937-046-2	£12.99
Devon	1-85937-052-7	£14.99
Dorset	1-85937-075-6	£14.99
Dorset Coast	1-85937-062-4	£14.99
Around Dublin	1-85937-058-6	£12.99
East Anglia	1-85937-059-4	£14.99
Around Eastbourne	1-85937-061-6	£12.99
English Castles	1-85937-078-0	£14.99
Around Falmouth	1-85937-066-7	£12.99
Hampshire	1-85937-064-0	£14.99
Isle of Man	1-85937-065-9	£14.99
Around Maidstone	1-85937-056-X	£12.99
North Yorkshire	1-85937-048-9	£14.99
Around Nottingham	1-85937-060-8	£12.99
Around Penzance	1-85937-069-1	£12.99
Around Reading	1-85937-087-X	£12.99
Around St Ives	1-85937-068-3	£12.99
Around Salisbury	1-85937-091-8	£12.99
Around Scarborough	1-85937-104-3	£12.99
Scottish Castles	1-85937-077-2	£14.99
Around Sevenoaks and Tonbridge	1-85937-057-8	£12.99

Sheffield and S Yorkshire	1-85937-070-5	£14.99
Shropshire	1-85937-083-7	£14.99
Staffordshire	1-85937-047-0 (96pp)	£12.99
Suffolk	1-85937-074-8	£14.99
Surrey	1-85937-081-0	£14.99
Around Torbay	1-85937-063-2	£12.99
Wiltshire	1-85937-053-5	£14.99
Around Bakewell	1-85937-113-2	£12.99
Around Bournemouth	1-85937-067-5	£12.99
Cambridgeshire	1-85937-086-1	£14.99
Essex	1-85937-082-9	£14.99
Around Great Yarmouth	1-85937-085-3	£12.99
Hertfordshire	1-85937-079-9	£14.99
Isle of Wight	1-85937-114-0	£14.99
Around Lincoln	1-85937-111-6	£12.99
Oxfordshire	1-85937-076-4	£14.99
Around Shrewsbury	1-85937-110-8	£12.99
South Devon Coast	1-85937-107-8	£14.99
Around Stratford upon Avon	1-85937-098-5	£12.99
West Midlands	1-85937-109-4	£14.99

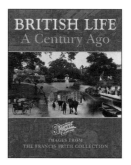

British Life A Century Ago
246 x 189mm
144pp, hardback.
Black and white
Lavishly illustrated with photos from the turn of the century, and with extensive commentary. It offers a unique insight into the social history and heritage of bygone Britain.

1-85937-103-5 £17.99

Available from your local bookshop or from the publisher

Around Bath	1-85937-097-7	£12.99	Mar
Cumbria	1-85937-101-9	£14.99	Mar
Down the Thames	1-85937-121-3	£14.99	Mar
Around Exeter	1-85937-126-4	£12.99	Mar
Greater Manchester	1-85937-108-6	£14.99	Mar
Around Harrogate	1-85937-112-4	£12.99	Mar
Around Leicester	1-85937-073-x	£12.99	Mar
Around Liverpool	1-85937-051-9	£12.99	Mar
Northumberland and Tyne & Wear			
	1-85937-072-1	£14.99	Mar
Around Oxford	1-85937-096-9	£12.99	Mar
Around Plymouth	1-85937-119-1	£12.99	Mar
Around Southport	1-85937-106-x	£12.99	Mar
Welsh Castles	1-85937-120-5	£14.99	Mar
Canals and Waterways	1-85937-129-9	£17.99	Apr
Around Guildford	1-85937-117-5	£12.99	Apr
Around Horsham	1-85937-127-2	£12.99	Apr
Around Ipswich	1-85937-133-7	£12.99	Apr
Ireland (pb)	1-85937-181-7	£9.99	Apr
London (pb)	1-85937-183-3	£9.99	Apr
New Forest	1-85937-128-0	£14.99	Apr
Around Newark	1-85937-105-1	£12.99	Apr
Around Newquay	1-85937-140-x	£12.99	Apr
Scotland (pb)	1-85937-182-5	£9.99	Apr
Around Southampton	1-85937-088-8	£12.99	Apr
Sussex (pb)	1-85937-184-1	£9.99	Apr
Around Winchester	1-85937-139-6	£12.99	Apr
Around Belfast	1-85937-094-2	£12.99	May
Colchester (pb)	1-85937-188-4	£8.99	May
Exmoor	1-85937-132-9	£14.99	May
Leicestershire (pb)	1-85937-185-x	£9.99	May
Lincolnshire	1-85937-135-3	£14.99	May
North Devon Coast	1-85937-146-9	£14.99	May
Nottinghamshire (pb)	1-85937-187-6	£9.99	May
Peak District	1-85937-100-0	£14.99	May
Around Truro	1-85937-147-7	£12.99	May
Yorkshire (pb)	1-85937-186-8	£9.99	May
Berkshire (pb)	1-85937-191-4	£9.99	Jun
Brighton (pb)	1-85937-192-2	£8.99	Jun
County Durham	1-85937-123-x	£14.99	Jun
Dartmoor	1-85937-145-0	£14.99	Jun
Down the Severn	1-85937-118-3	£14.99	Jun
East London	1-85937-080-2	£14.99	Jun
East Sussex	1-85937-130-2	£14.99	Jun
Glasgow (pb)	1-85937-190-6	£8.99	Jun
Kent (pb)	1-85937-189-2	£9.99	Jun
Kent Living Memories	1-85937-125-6	£14.99	Jun
Redhill to Reigate	1-85937-137-x	£12.99	Jun
Stone Circles & Ancient Monuments			
	1-85937-143-4	£17.99	Jun
Victorian & Edwardian Kent			
	1-85937-149-3	£14.99	Jun
Victorian & Edwardian Maritime Album			
	1-85937-144-2	£17.99	Jun
Victorian & Edwardian Yorkshire			
	1-85937-154-x	£14.99	Jun
West Sussex	1-85937-148-5	£14.99	Jun
Churches of Berkshire	1-85937-170-1	£17.99	Jul
Churches of Dorset	1-85937-172-8	£17.99	Jul
Derbyshire (pb)	1-85937-196-5	£9.99	Jul
Edinburgh (pb)	1-85937-193-0	£8.99	Jul
Folkstone	1-85937-124-8	£12.99	Jul
Gloucestershire	1-85937-102-7	£14.99	Jul
Herefordshire	1-85937-174-4	£14.99	Jul
North London	1-85937-206-6	£14.99	Jul
Norwich (pb)	1-85937-194-9	£8.99	Jul
Ports and Harbours	1-85937-208-2	£17.99	Jul
Somerset and Avon	1-85937-153-1	£14.99	Jul
South Devon Living Memories			
	1-85937-168-x	£14.99	Jul
Warwickshire (pb)	1-85937-203-1	£9.99	Jul
Worcestershire	1-85937-152-3	£14.99	Jul
Yorkshire Living Memories			
	1-85937-166-3	£14.99	Jul

FRITH PRODUCTS & SERVICES

Francis Frith would doubtless be pleased to know that the pioneering publishing venture he started in 1860 still continues today. More than a hundred and thirty years later, The Francis Frith Collection continues in the same innovative tradition and is now one of the foremost publishers of vintage photographs in the world. Some of the current activities include:

Interior Decoration

Today Frith's photographs can be seen framed and as giant wall murals in thousands of pubs, restaurants, hotels, banks, retail stores and other public buildings throughout the country. In every case they enhance the unique local atmosphere of the places they depict and provide reminders of gentler days in an increasingly busy and frenetic world.

Product Promotions

Frith products have been used by many major companies to promote the sales of their own products or to reinforce their own history and heritage. Brands include Hovis bread, Courage beers, Scots Porage Oats, Colman's mustard, Cadbury's foods, Mellow Birds coffee, Dunhill pipe tobacco, Guinness, and Bulmer's Cider.

Genealogy and Family History

As the interest in family history and roots grows world-wide, more and more people are turning to Frith's photographs of Great Britain for images of the towns, villages and streets where their ancestors lived; and, of course, photographs of the churches and chapels where their ancestors were christened, married and buried are an essential part of every genealogy tree and family album.

A series of easy-to-use CD Roms is planned for publication, and an increasing number of Frith photographs will be able to be viewed on specialist genealogy sites. A growing range of Frith books will be available on CD.

The Internet

Already thousands of Frith photographs can be viewed and purchased on the internet. By the end of the year 2000 some 60,000 Frith photographs will be available on the internet. The number of sites is constantly expanding, each focussing on different products and services from the Collection.

Some of the sites are listed below.

www.townpages.co.uk
www.icollector.com
www.barclaysquare.co.uk
www.cornwall-online.co.uk

For background information on the Collection look at the three following sites:

www.francisfrith.com
www.francisfrith.co.uk
www.frithbook.co.uk

Frith Products

All Frith photographs are available Framed or just as Mounted Prints, and can be ordered from the address below. From time to time other products - Address Books, Calendars, Table Mats, etc - are available.

For further information:
if you would like further information on any of the above aspects of the Frith business please contact us at the address below:
The Francis Frith Collection,
Frith's Barn, Teffont, Salisbury, Wiltshire,
England SP3 5QP.
Tel: +44 (0)1722 716 376 Fax: +44 (0)1722 716 881 Email: uksales@francisfrith.com

---

To receive your FREE Mounted Print

Mounted Print
Overall size 14 x 11 inches

Cut out this Voucher and return it with your remittance for £1.50 to cover postage and handling. Choose any photograph included in this book. Your SEPIA print will be A4 in size, and mounted in a cream mount with burgundy rule lines, overall size 14 x 11 inches.

Order additional Mounted Prints at HALF PRICE (only £7.49 each*)

If there are further pictures you would like to order, possibly as gifts for friends and family, acquire them at half price (no additional postage and handling required).

Have your Mounted Prints framed*

For an additional £14.95 per print you can have your chosen Mounted Print framed in an elegant polished wood and gilt moulding, overall size 16 x 13 inches (no additional postage and handling required).

---

* IMPORTANT!
These special prices are only available if ordered using the original voucher on this page (no copies permitted) and at the same time as your free Mounted Print, for delivery to the same address

---

Frith Collectors' Guild

From time to time we publish a magazine of news and stories about Frith photographs and further special offers of Frith products. If you would like 12 months FREE membership, please return this form.

Send completed forms to:
**The Francis Frith Collection,
Frith's Barn, Teffont, Salisbury,
Wiltshire SP3 5QP**

Voucher for FREE and Reduced Price Frith Prints

Picture no.	Page number	Qty	Mounted @ £7.49	Framed + £14.95	Total Cost
		1	**Free of charge***	£	£
			£7.49	£	£
			£7.49	£	£
			£7.49	£	£
			£7.49	£	£
			£7.49	£	£
			* Post & handling		£1.50
Book Title			**Total Order Cost**		£

Please do not photocopy this voucher. Only the original is valid, so please cut it out and return it to us.

I enclose a cheque / postal order for £ . . . .
made payable to 'The Francis Frith Collection'
OR please debit my Mastercard / Visa / Switch / Amex card

Number . . . .

Expires . . . . Signature . . . .

Name Mr/Mrs/Ms . . . .

Address . . . .

. . . .

. . . .

. . . .

. . . . Postcode . . . .

Daytime Tel No . . . .   Valid to 31/12/01

The Francis Frith Collectors' Guild

Please enrol me as a member for 12 months free of charge.

Name Mr/Mrs/Ms . . . .

Address . . . .

. . . .

. . . .

. . . . Postcode . . . .